SEA GLASS HUNTER'S HANDBOOK

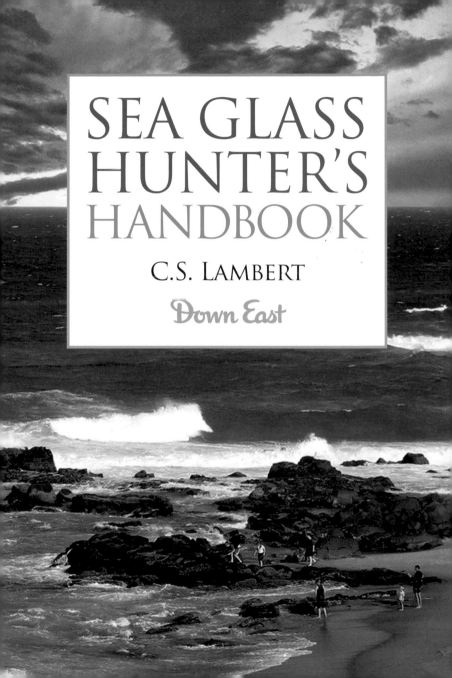

SEA GLASS HUNTER'S HANDBOOK

C.S. LAMBERT

Down East

Text Copyright © 2010 by Carole Lambert

Photo Copyright individual photographers

All rights reserved.

ISBN 978-0-89272-910-4

Design by Lynda Chilton

Back cover photo by Pembroke S. Bryant

Front cover photo by Tina Lam

Printed at Oceanic Graphic Printing

5　4　3

BOOKS·MAGAZINE·ONLINE
www.downeast.com

Distributed to the trade by National Book Network

Library of Congress Cataloging-in-Publication Data

Lambert, C. S. (Carole S.), 1953-

　Sea glass hunter's handbook / by C.S. Lambert.

　　　p. cm.

　ISBN 978-0-89272-910-4

　1. Sea glass. I. Title.

　NK5439.S34L35 2010

　748--dc22

　　　　　　　　　　　2010018398

Beaches change every day,
and sea glass comes and goes
with the tide. For those who have
a deep primitive attraction to the
ocean, looking at sea glass in a
jar, or touching an individual piece
carried in a pocket, triggers seaside
memories of salty brine
and crashing waves.

Photo by Pembroke S. Bryant, Kill Devil Hills, NC

CONTENTS

THE WORLD OF SEA GLASS

The world of sea glass is bigger than you think. People all over the world collect it, there are dozens of websites dedicated to it, and international conventions are devoted entirely to finding and identifying it. There is something about these shards of glass and ceramic that have been tossed around by the tides that captures the imagination. Maybe it's the way that nature takes something mundane, like a broken bottle, and turns it into something beautiful. Maybe it is the connection to the past. Maybe it's the immediate associations sea glass brings of time by the ocean, the waves, the salty smell of brine. Whatever the reason, sea glass is a thriving and colorful subject to explore.

My Favorite Find

The stopper was found by my friend Paul. When I started 'hunting' about 8 years ago, it was something

I tended to do on my own; when Paul started to come with me, he got addicted, too. This was a sunny, crisp, cold January day at a lovely pebble beach just south of Aberdeen, and guess who got the 'find of the day,' yes, the 'assistant!' Definitely a happy-dance occasion for Paul (and me!). It's the only nearly complete stopper we have, and sits on the window ledge catching the sun with all the other special pieces. Sea glass hunting has proved to be a great way of spending relaxing, quality time together, even if it does get a bit competitive sometimes.

—Anne Dunbar, Aberdeen, UK

What is sea glass?

Sea glass is fragments of indeterminate glass and ceramic objects that have been in oceans or rivers for incalculable amounts of time, have taken on the scars of their untold voyages, and have washed up on beaches everywhere. Some collectors consider it more precious than gemstones. Others find a trajectory into history. Sea glass may be appreciated for its singular beauty or dismissed as litter. This is why I love it so much.

Photo by Linda Jereb, Sebastian, FL

Multi: remnant from a glassblower's pipe discarded in the manufacturer's ocean or riverside dump.

Art² x Nature² = Sea Glass

Art is subjective. Sometimes the evolution of an idea to a finished work belongs solely to the artist. Sometimes it results from collaboration. Sometimes no one, including the artist, knows how the finished work got there in the first place. Most would have to agree that it is considered art to someone.

Photo by Tami Ewing, Renton, WA

This sea glass cairn is a fitting tribute to the ocean.

But sea glass is art on its own terms. It is complex and simple, fragile but sturdy at the same time.

Some pieces have color where there seems to be none. Some shine as prisms and others are opaque. Some are considered valueless, others priceless.

When these fragments emerge on a beach somewhere, each is unique as a fingerprint.

My Favorite Find

My sons have gotten used to my passion for sea glass, and will even accompany me on a hunt occasionally. This piece was found by one of my sons in Seaside, CA. He was sand-boarding (riding snowboards on sand dunes) and came across a big pile of glass. He picked this piece out for me. I remember having 7-Up out of bottles when I was a kid, and their motto "You like it, and it likes you." It was a sweet and special gift, and I was pleased to add it to my collection.

—Melinda Vahradian, Santa Cruz, CA

Pebbles, rocks, and rock formations often trap prime sea glass and shards.

Sea Glass Hunter's Handbook

If you are reading this book, most likely: 1) you are passionate about sea glass and it has an important place in your life; 2) you might not be a devotee, but you enjoy scanning the beach for sea glass or 3) you don't know much about sea glass, but you are interested in finding out. If you are in the second or third category, we'll have you gearing up and seaglunking like a pro in no time. If you are in category one, you already know what I'm writing about.

Admit it. As a serious sea glass collector, you've probably thought of extending your beachcombing into the night by creating a headlamp that could illuminate a small beach.

Photo by JoAnna Forrester, Lincolnshire, UK

This sea glass marble resembles a full moon, and its well-hydrated surface mimics Lunar cycles.

You might add optical lenses with a retractable arm that zooms in and out on individual pieces of sea glass.

Probably the result of scuttled ballast, marbles are highly sought after by seaglunkers.

And when temperatures exceed 90 degrees, a safari hat with a small solar-powered fan directed to your forehead would come in handy.

You are not alone with these thoughts.

No matter who you are, anyone can appreciate the evocative beauty of sea glass, and in the *Sea Glass Hunter's Handbook* you'll find everything an expert sea-glunker needs to know about the world and wonders of sea glass. ⋌

Many seaglunkers prefer porcelain, china, and pottery shards to sea glass.

SEA GLASS ORIGINS

Who knows how or why a fragment of glass or china lands on a beach? Shipwrecks and dumpsites seem to be the most common source of transformation from whole to broken object. The occasional plate or bottle jettisoned from a restaurant, houses swept out to sea, ballast dumped in ports also contribute to the cause. Whatever the reasons—some unknown—small, chaffed pieces of history survive.

Shipwrecks

Art and literature often romanticize the truth behind shipwrecks. While legendary pirates, allegedly, growled "aargh," often with a parrot on

Three-masted bark Annie C. Maguire *ran ashore in 1886 at Portland Head Light, Cape Elizabeth, ME.*

their shoulder, real lives were lost and fortunes scuttled when ships went down.

Incalculable shipwrecks from centuries past dot the world's oceans and rivers. Typhoons, icebergs, reefs, sandbanks, and lightening took captains by surprise, and navigational errors and narrow shipping channels brought down even the sturdiest ships. Whether 16th century Spanish galleons carrying gold or 19th century clippers running supplies to unilat-

Glass fragments in the evolutionary stages of sea glass: sharp and shiny to mildly abraded to perfectly hydrated.

eral countries, large concentrations of shipwrecks can be traced through international trade routes.

Shattered and buffeted by ocean travels, sea glass and other artifacts continue to wash up from these wrecks around the globe and offer a compelling look into earlier centuries, when the world was thought flat and cartographers marked "Here Be Monsters" on paper seas.

The Dry Salvages

These ships, and many others unrecorded, have wrecked on a small group of rocks, known as "the dry salvages," three-quarters of a mile off the shores of

SHIPWRECKS IN
ROCKPORT, MA HARBOR

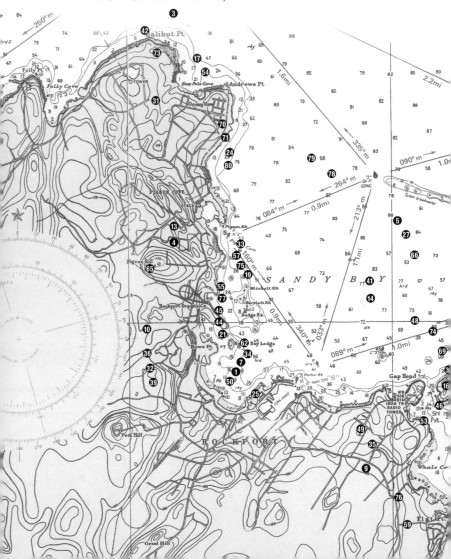

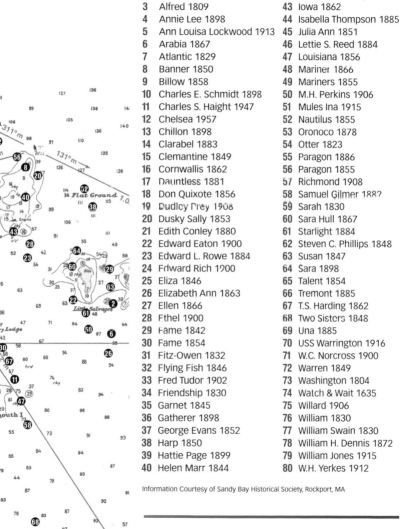

1	Ada F. Lowe 1867	41	Henry M. Stanley 1899
2	Adien 1856	42	Henry B. Withington 1990
3	Alfred 1809	43	Iowa 1862
4	Annie Lee 1898	44	Isabella Thompson 1885
5	Ann Louisa Lockwood 1913	45	Julia Ann 1851
6	Arabia 1867	46	Lettie S. Reed 1884
7	Atlantic 1829	47	Louisiana 1856
8	Banner 1850	48	Mariner 1866
9	Billow 1858	49	Mariners 1855
10	Charles E. Schmidt 1898	50	M.H. Perkins 1906
11	Charles S. Haight 1947	51	Mules Ina 1915
12	Chelsea 1957	52	Nautilus 1855
13	Chillon 1898	53	Oronoco 1878
14	Clarabel 1883	54	Otter 1823
15	Clemantine 1849	55	Paragon 1886
16	Cornwallis 1862	56	Paragon 1855
17	Dauntless 1881	57	Richmond 1908
18	Don Quixote 1856	58	Samuel Gilmer 1882
19	Dudley Prey 1908	59	Sarah 1830
20	Dusky Sally 1853	60	Sara Hull 1867
21	Edith Conley 1880	61	Starlight 1884
22	Edward Eaton 1900	62	Steven C. Phillips 1848
23	Edward L. Rowe 1884	63	Susan 1847
24	Edward Rich 1900	64	Sara 1898
25	Eliza 1846	65	Talent 1854
26	Elizabeth Ann 1863	66	Tremont 1885
27	Ellen 1866	67	T.S. Harding 1862
28	Ethel 1900	68	Two Sisters 1848
29	Fame 1842	69	Una 1885
30	Fame 1854	70	USS Warrington 1916
31	Fitz-Owen 1832	71	W.C. Norcross 1900
32	Flying Fish 1846	72	Warren 1849
33	Fred Tudor 1902	73	Washington 1804
34	Friendship 1830	74	Watch & Wait 1635
35	Garnet 1845	75	Willard 1906
36	Gatherer 1898	76	William 1830
37	George Evans 1852	77	William Swain 1830
38	Harp 1850	78	William H. Dennis 1872
39	Hattie Page 1899	79	William Jones 1915
40	Helen Marr 1844	80	W.H. Yerkes 1912

Information Courtesy of Sandy Bay Historical Society, Rockport, MA

Rockport, MA. This, no doubt, explains the great number of sea glass fragments that still wash up on Rockport's Front Beach. Inspired by these wrecks, T.S. Eliot wrote "The Dry Salvages," a stanza in his 1941 poem "The Four Quartets":

The river is within us, the sea is all about us;
The sea is the land's edge also, the granite
Into which it reaches, the beaches where it tosses

Its hints of earlier and other creation:
The starfish, the horseshoe crab,
The whale's backbone;

The Pools where it offers to our curiosity
The more delicate algae and the sea anemone.
It tosses up our losses, the torn seine,
The shattered lobsterpot, the broken oar
And the gear of foreign dead men.
The sea has many voices,

Many gods and many voices.

My Favorite Find

I was on the way back to my car from treasure hunting a favorite beach and I was thinking about my dad
(he's been gone for 20 years now) and our family vaca-
tions. My favorites would be when we
would go to the ocean and camp. I
was missing him and just walking and
remembering when I saw just the tip
of the shard. I almost walked past it,
but stopped, brushed the sand away,
and there it was. A perfect heart. I
know a lot of people would say it was
just a coincidence, but I like to think
it was my dad letting me know he was
thinking about me, too.

I've heard other people with the same story, so it's
not unique, but I know the love they were feeling when
they found their special piece of sea glass. So I've used
my sea glass heart in a lot of my pictures to remember
and honor my dad, making it one of my all-time favorite
pieces of sea glass.

—Tami Ewing, Renton, WA

The *Severn*

In 2004, large numbers of sea glass and shards appeared on Lewes Beach in Lewes, Delaware. This led to the discovery of a 1774 shipwreck believed to be

Photo by Marilyn Boyles, Meadville, PA

the *Severn,* a 200-ton British merchant ship.

The wreck site has been placed on the National Register of Historic Places, and therefore, is off-limits to the public. Archaeologists, historians, and volunteers have examined more than 45,000 artifacts that open a window to civilization 300 years ago. According to researchers, the ship and its cargo, which included china, bottles of mineral water, and pipes, had been insured by Lloyd's of London.

Bonfire Glass.

C.S.S. *Alabama*

In 1864, part of the American Civil War played out in the waters between England and France. Of the thousands of ships that lie on the bottom of the English

Channel, one of them, the C.S.S. *Alabama*, carries ghosts that still haunt the English, French, and Americans today.

The extraordinary battle of the C.S.S. *Alabama* took place within view of 17,000 spectators, who were in Cherbourg, France, to celebrate the opening of a new casino. The *Alabama* was defeated by the U.S.S. *Kearsarge* on a mission to disrupt supplies from reaching America.

The *Alabama*'s Staffordshire toilet basins and the captain's china are among the artifacts recovered that were driven by the Channel's strong currents.

Coastal Dumpsites

The humble lackluster sister of shipwrecks, the coastal dump, offers up ocean-side Cinderellas. Plain old garbage, including once useful glass and china objects thrown out with potato peelings and coffee grounds, turns into highly coveted sea glass. The notion of garbage, however unappealing, creates an unexpected variety of treasure—from porcelain doll fragments to chunks of crystal to a broken plate revealing an image that is nothing short of a miniature masterpiece.

Sea glass and ceramic shards often blend with the environment.

*Discarded bottle that might become
sea glass many years in the future.*

Many island communities still schedule trash days, unwisely utilizing the ocean as a solution for waste disposal. A variation on this general dumping, a different evolutionary stage for dumpsite sea glass, is trash burnt in bonfires before being jettisoned. Bonfires change the fragments' chemical composition, giving them condensed, sometimes folded or pebbly, features.

Restaurants and Bars

Who doesn't love a harborside restaurant or bar? Sea gulls and flip-flops. Seafood and beer. Checkered plastic tablecloths. Look down at the sand between

Array of sea glass including rare colors: red, teal, cobalt, lime.

pilings and you might find a blinding reflection of not-ready-to-pick-up sea glass, which recalls spring breaks in Daytona Beach. Whether customers discreetly fling china plates over the deck in a solitary game of frizbee, or waiters chuck empty bottles into the harbor, so begins the journey for whole objects destined to become sea glass with an identifiable past.

My Favorite Find

First I smell that smell and am overcome with a

sensation of elation. Like a tight faucet turned open, everything floods from me. I scan the view, take a deep breath, and inevitably utter, "God, I love it here." I stride quickly to where the sand is still wet from the previous tide and then, and then I am gone. There is no thinking, just being. I have no awareness of time or of myself. If I am searching for glass, it is rote, with no more or less consciousness than a jellyfish searching for sustenance. It is not mindlessness or oblivion, as I am wholly aware, but in a way that preempts any reality outside of the moment. There I am seaweed, I am water, I am stone, I am fish. I am a grain of sand, warm in the sun. I am reduced to nothing, but part of everything. I am home, I am free, I am one with the sea, I am the primordial me, and the glass is just my excuse to be there.

—Sherry Fields, Friendship, ME

Coastal Interuptors, Factories, and Ballast

Any sort of coastal devastation, such as erosion and dramatic weather conditions, can propel objects into the ocean that might turn into sea glass.

For sea glass hunters on a mission, nothing compares to a glass or china factory seaside disposal outlet. Consider the volume of cast-offs evolving into perfectly hydrated rounds and ovals, many with combined or fused colors. This is Val Halla for aficionados

Ships, especially during the China Trade, often carried inexpensive glass or china products as ballast, which was ejected into harbors before goods were loaded for the return trip.

Looking for sea glass at Coney Island at the turn of the 20th century wasn't a good idea then, nor is it now.

WAYS OF SEEING SEA GLASS

First, When?

Sun, oh glorious sun. The rays stream down, freeing the mind's clutter. Regardless the season, solar energy is invigorating, but should be harnessed with sunscreen and preferably a hat.

And, the moon can change your life. An indispensible site, www.moonconnection.com, has a calendar that calculates phases of the moon day by day, year by year, around the world. And that is very useful indeed for sea glass hunters. But there's more. Here you'll also find the best lunar conditions for fishing. This site explains the 1969 moon-landing hoax. There is a virtual

Whitby, North Yorkshire, UK

moon store where you can buy movie posters of the human obsession with vampires. And here's the biggest tip of all from moonconnection.com: Their article "Trading by the Light of the Moon" deciphers the best time to buy and sell on the stock market according to the phases of the moon. Really, I'm not kidding. This is a serious site with scholarly research and charts.

And Why Is This Important To a Sea Glass Hunter?

Simply put, you've got your gravity and your celestial bodies. The bigger the moon appears, the higher and lower the tides. So, a big full moon, aided by a powerful storm, during low tide = sea glass nirvana. In coastal towns, tide charts are often available in hardware stores, banks, or stores specializing in fishing and boating gear. Also see: tidesandcurrents.noaa.gov/faq2.html.

Now Where?

Beautiful, sandy, expansive beaches are sometimes not good sea glass turf. Look instead for inner harbors, former coastal dump and factory sites, beaches near known shipwrecks, river mouths, and residential areas with severe storm damage.

Sandy versus pebbly versus rocky. High tidemark versus low tidemark and mid-tidemark. It's an individual

Extreme seaglunking. John Boyles didn't notice the wave behind him. He looked up and asked his wife if it was raining.

choice, but most beachcombers agree that a wrack line—a horizontal line of pebbles and other debris—traps sea glass.

Of course, beaches are fickle mistresses that can whip up piles of contradictions.

And, of Course, How?

Most seasoned beachcombers have honed their individual skills for the hunt. Walking forward, turning around, and covering the same ground in the opposite direction seems to be the most popular method.

Then there are the zig-zaggers.

And the sitters, who are often diggers.

The rock rollers and boulder perusers.

In his book Pure Sea Glass *Richard LaMotte identifies probable sea glass origins by color.*

"You are my blue beach glass."

Some avoid shadows.

Others search only in the shadows or on cloudy days.

Many combine all of these methods, and, of course, it's a good idea to look up and out toward the ocean every now and then.

And now for some general tips:

Tip One: Camouflage

Sometimes the most beautiful shards hide in unexpected places. The ever-illusive china and porcelain doll parts—arms, ears, partial faces—might disguise themselves as shells. Body parts from many types of dolls are found all over the world. Their demise is attributed to being thrown away, but more commonly they are shipwreck survivors.

Intricately patterned transferware shards also blend with elements on a beach, and it is worth taking a second look. Blue Staffordshire shards mingle easily with mussel shells, and brown transferware might hide among pebbles.

Clay pipe stems are often overlooked because they appear to be bits of seine netting or small metal tubes.

Photo by C.S. Lambert, Owls Head, ME

My Favorite Find

I found this pottery piece on one of the beaches on Cheung Chau Island, one of the many islands of Hong Kong. According to books about old Hong Kong, that island functioned as a shipyard and trading post for seafaring vessels of SE Asia almost a century ago. These activities went on right on that beach, where I found most of my treasures.

I found this almost three years ago, when I was strolling along the 'rubble line' looking for sea glass, pottery, and seashells. I saw this one, face down in the sand. Back side stained and edges worn smooth, it looked just like a very old piece of seashell. I realized it was a face only after I got home, when I was cleaning and sorting my 'loot'!

As I studied it, I realized that it was the face of the 'monkey god' in Chinese folklore who made a monk's pilgrimage to India, accompanied by three of his apprentices, and fought off bad spirits on their treacherous journey. Everyone loves this 'monkey god' for his playfulness and love of justice.

The picture shows the face amongst a jigsaw of plain white pottery pieces, showing how easily it might have been missed!

—Tina Lam, Hong Kong

Clay pipe fashioned after Charles Dickens' character Wilkins Micawber, from David Copperfield.

The majority of beached pipes originated in England and were sent to foreign ports in cargo containers. Pipe stems averaged 8 ½" long and pipes were often smoked communally, each person snapping off the tip after using it and then throwing it overboard.

Finding a pipe's age depends on the stem's bore size, which decreases roughly ¹⁄₆₄" every 30 years. For example, the diameter of a bore measuring $\frac{8}{64}$" dates a pipe between 1620 and 1650, while the diameter of a bore measuring $\frac{7}{64}$" dates a pipe between 1650 and 1680.

Tip Two: Tools of the Trade

If you are a purist beachcomber, you probably walk the beach unencumbered. However, you might want to consider one or all of the following accoutrements. Summer: hat with attached fan, sunglasses, fishing vest,

Photo by C.S. Lambert, Owls Head, ME

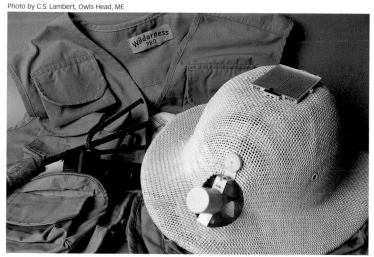

Seaglunking gear: vest with many pockets, hoe, flashlight, safari hat with solar-powered fan.

sunscreen, long-handled grabber, hoe, rubber gloves for particularly nasty areas, pad and pencil for rampant poetic thoughts.

Additional winter accessories: fingerless gloves, thermos with hot water to melt ice-covered pieces, antique glove-stretcher for picking up cold, wet pieces.

Some believe that wintertime beachcombing offers the finest sea glass and shards.

My Favorite Find

My family has a cabin in the redwoods just south of the town where I found this marble, so I have driven by the beach dozens of times each year for my entire life. We were going down for spring break with family and friends. It was my birthday and I decided to sneak away at low tide on my favorite

beach. It is not an easy place to hunt for sea glass. The ocean is frigid and rough even on the mildest of days. I got slammed by waves a couple of times before I decided to get serious and change into my wetsuit and booties. I still ended up freezing and after a couple of hours had to stop because my hands and feet were numb. A young man I met there told me that just the week before a woman who was looking for sea glass got pulled out to sea. Fortunately she was rescued by the Coast Guard within half an hour. It was worth the risk though, as you can see from "my new favorite." Truly a gift from the sea!

—Sharon Sand, Belvedere Tiburon, CA

Tip Three: Far from Home

Finding fertile sea glass beaches in foreign territory is a dodgy job. Here are some suggestions:

- Assume that there is a local doctrine: "Strangers must be monitored."

- Visit the local welcome center or chamber of commerce. Don't ask right away about your mission. Question a staff member about good restaurants and accommodations, then slip in, "How are the beaches here? My sister asked me to bring back some sea glass as a souvenir."

- Don't wear clothes that are too bright or too new. This applies especially to tennis shoes.

- Walk casually, never refer to a map or stop strangers in the street with questions.

- Avoid lobster shacks where other tourists might be working on the same beachcombing strategies as you.

- Pretend that you are from a land-locked state or country, and that you've never heard of sea glass.

- Befriend one of the locals and buy him or her a few glasses of wine or beer. Remember the WWII missive that can work in your favor, "Loose lips sink ships." ✐

Photo by Londi Colton, Port Angeles, WA

A BEACH-COMBER'S LEXICON

One might ask when the term "sea glass" was first used? Well, if Geoffrey Chaucer ever mentioned sea glass, the *Oxford English Dictionary* didn't pick up on it.

In the meantime, definitions of sea glass and related words keep cropping up and merging with other expressions. "Sea glass" has its own following, but "beach glass" lobbyists are equally adamant. Are sea glass and beach glass actually the same thing?

The short answer is it's hard to say.

Here are some terms and definitions that might clarify or confuse beachcombers of any level of expertise.

A beachcomber's tribute to the ocean.

Art Glass: combinations of colored glass

Backstamp: a maker's name or identifying mark, sometimes including approximate date of manufacture

Beach, Ocean, or Riverbank: resting place for sea glass

Beach Glass: same as sea glass; alternative definition: glass that washed up on riverbanks; glass with little or no hydration

Blue Willow: most popular china pattern in the history of dinnerware; made by approximately 150 potters from 13 countries; still manufactured today

Shard possibly from a Victorian-era Staffordshire teapot or bowl.

Bonfire Glass: glass altered by campfire or dump fire, often entrapping sand or other small objects

Bottles, Messages In: while amusing, they are not sea glass

Cairn: a mound of stones or sea glass erected as a landmark or memorial

My Favorite Find

I really love the deep aqua colour of these saki bottle fragments. I have loved sea glass ever since I was a kid.

 In fact I collected everything I found at the beach, not realising how special it was until I bought a beach house. It was as if the beach was inviting me to this new journey in my life. I all of a sudden realised that my obsession to collect sea glass, although not very common in Greece, was really a particular hobby and even business for lots of people around the world, and it made me soon a member of a very big creative community. What I particularly love about sea glass is the anticipation to find a new wonderful piece, the walk at the beach enclosed in my thoughts, the hunt. Just like the trip to Ithaca is much more interesting than the destination itself.

—Ariadne Skyrianidou. Thessaloniki, Greece

Cameo Glass: two colors fused together with intricate carved design

China Trade: network of oceanic trade routes

Chinoisery: a European style inspired by the East, which dominated art and design in the late 17th century

Clay Pipes: stems or bowls, sometimes a whole pipe, dating primarily from the 1500s to the 1800s

Clinkers, Clunkers: fragments that need to be thrown back in the ocean

Codd: marble enclosed in a bottle neck instead of a cork, to seal in carbonation; made from the late 1800s to the early 1900s

Collector: seaglasser, seaglunker, treasurer hunter, mudlark, oceanic archaeologist

Composition: primarily sand, soda, lime

Cooked, Not: sharp edges, shiny areas; needs to be cast back into the ocean for further cooking

Crazing: network of fine lines caused by a ceramic body and glaze expanding and contracting at different rates

Current: steady onward movement of water

Cut Glass: glass decorated with facets that are cut or ground

Debris: not sea glass

Doll Parts: china or porcelain fragments of arms, legs, heads, etc. from dolls or statuettes

End-of-Day Glass: flecked or swirled with another color, usually white; created by glass manufacturing workers with glass left over at the workday's end

Extreme Beachcombing: rappelling, diving, searching at night with car headlights pointed at beach; also see contraption proposed in chapter one

Factories: origins of sea glass and shards

Fake or Faux: glass mechanically or chemically altered to resemble sea glass, also called fantasy glass

Fiesta® Dinnerware: art deco–inspired chinaware designed in 1936 by the Homer Laughlin China Company

Flotsam: odds and ends, usually from wreckage or cargo spill, that float on water; not to be confused with jetsam

Flow Blue: blurry design that results from cobalt oxide applied to a porous plate and then fired

Found in Delaware Bay, this sea glass won 1st place in the Sea Glass Lovers' photo contest. It originated as a Hartmann & Fehrenback Brewing Co. embossed beer bottle. Photo by Michael Morrissey, Pine Hill, NJ

Frozen Charlottes: tiny porcelain dolls, ranging from ½" to 5 ½", that were often given away as premiums

Glass Beach: monumental amounts of sea glass on several beaches throughout the world, all named 'Glass Beach'

Handpainted tile fragment found in Rockport, MA.

Glass Floats: colorful glass balls strung together on fishnets for buoyancy; not considered sea glass

Harbor: resting place for sea glass

Holy Grail: orange sea glass

Homer Laughlin China Company: one of America's largest china manufacturers; started in 1871

Hydration: process of disintegration where glass takes on a pocked, opaque surface when left in saltwater for extended periods of time

Jadite: opaque pale-green glass popular in the 1930s

Jetsam: odds and ends that sank and have washed ashore; not to be confused with flotsam

Perfectly abraded glass mimics colors of the sea.

Kickup: also called push-up, or dimple; solid or hollow
indentation in bottle bottoms to create stability and
extra strength

Manganese: mineral that introduces yellow, red, and
purple to balance the naturally occurring blues and
greens in clear glass; when the glass is exposed to
sunlight, it turns to numerous shades of purple

Mocha Ware: created in the 1700s; bottom-of-the-line earthenware with a surface design created by using tobacco juice, hops, stale wine, and urine

Mother Nature: sea glass benefactor

Multi: scrap of fused, colored glass snapped off of a blow-pipe and discarded by an ocean-side manufacturer

Other Beach Treasures: shells, driftwood, Roman coins; usually ignored by serious sea glass aficionados

Pebbles, Rocks, Stones: sea glass waystations

Pressed Glass: molded designs in glass; an inexpensive version of cut glass

Pure Sea Glass: book written by Richard LaMotte, known as the godfather of sea glass

Rare Colors: orange, red, turquoise, yellow, darkest green known as "black glass," teal, gray

Registration of Designs Act: not enforced in England until 1842; prior to that, illustrations could be used freely without acknowledging the artist; most commonly used artists included Antoine Watteau and Thomas Gainsborough

A consummate beachcomber, Ginger prefers searching for sticks, plastic bottles, and rope. Here in Nags Head, NC, she settled for sea glass. Photo by Marilyn Boyles, Meadville, PA

Rounds: whole or fragments of bottle bottoms; also can be square, rectangular, or oval

Royal Warrant: heraldry of reigning monarch given to endorse goods and services supplied to royal family

Sand: medium where sea glass is most often found

Scene: fragment of a rare piece of china, pottery, etc. that depicts pastoral images; the rarest include a combination of land, sea, people, and/or animals

Sea Glass: aka mermaid's tears, lucky tears, ocean glass, sand glass, and the less poetic trash glass

Seaglunking: the combination of sea glass and spelunking

Seeding: throwing glass or ceramic shards that are not cooked enough or are too new into the ocean in order to create sea glass for future generations

Shards: ceramic fragments, aka sherds, chards, sea pottery, sea porcelain, sea china

Shells: sometimes resemble doll fragments

Slag Glass: opaque glass, usually white, with a second color running through

Stick: useful tool for flipping over shards

My Favorite Find

I lost my 'marbles' when my father died, coming so soon after my treatment for cancer. I was shell-shocked.

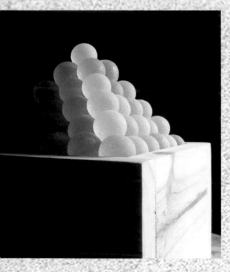

I held a small ceremony down on the shore of the River Humber's industrial banks. My son wandered along the shore with our dog to give me some privacy, and when we met up he handed me a 'Codd.' I spent the rest of the summer looking for marbles, and I really felt my 'Pop' was there with me, helping me come to terms with his death.

—Jo Forrester, Moortown, UK

Stippling: tiny dots applied to an engraved ceramic design to create the illusion of density or shading

Stoneware: a heavy, nonporous pottery, such as crockery

Storm: an event that usually brings an abundance of sea glass

Summer: too many tourists on the beach

Transferware/Transferprinting: technique invented in the mid-1700s whereby designs were engraved onto copper plates, transferred to paper, pressed onto soft-paste porcelain and pottery, and then fired to seal the surface

Wrack Line, or Tidal Wrack: a line of jetsam parallel to the shore between the low and high tides

Zen: philosophy for collectors. If you look for it you will not find it

Glass Beach, Bermuda
Photo by Debby Boone, Hagerstown, MD

5

LAWS: LIFE'S A BEACH

When is a beach open to the public? That depends on whom you talk to.

A New Jersey advocacy group, the Citizens Right to Access Beaches, or CRAB, invoked the nationwide Public Trust Doctrine, which originated in Roman times, circa 560. Accordingly, the state serves as trustee for the public and guarantees that their ownership begins at a beach's high tide mark.

However, in 1647 the Massachusetts Legislature transferred beach proprietorship to coastal property owners. This law also includes the state of Maine, which was, at the time, a district of

While rare, glass bottle stoppers and lavender sea glass are found around the world.

Massachusetts. That is, beaches are privately owned between the high and low water tidemarks. No frizbee, no walking, no beach blanket bingo allowed for the general public.

This law, still in place in 2010, was challenged in Maine's Supreme Court. Families have illegally trodden these beaches for centuries, which contemporary beachcombers claim has evolved into common law. Common law, they argue, trumps private access.

Another advocacy group, the Los Angeles Urban Rangers, conducts "sand safaris" in hopes of clarifying legal, safe, and environmentally appropriate access to California's beaches.

Armed with tape measures, easement maps, and a copy of the state's Constitution, the Urban Rangers test the public vs. private limits. But high and low tide marks, eminent domain, and vertical and lateral access-ways create a hornet's nest of boundaries. For now, many California beachcombers stay on wet sand areas, which are loosely considered public domain but are still hotly contested.

Public access to beaches on Michigan's Great Lakes is also unclear. One Michigan court official referred to Wisconsin's interpretation of the Public Trust Doctrine, and the definition of the high water mark:

"[T]he presence and action of the water is so continuous as to leave a distinct mark either by erosion, destruction of terrestrial vegetation, or other easily recognized characteristics." Public beach supporters use the term "easily recognized characteristics" to their advantage.

Incredible as it might seem, there are at least three beaches in the world that have veritable carpets of sea glass: Ft. Bragg, CA; St. George, Bermuda; and here: Kauai, HI.

And in Florida, members of the Surfrider Foundation point out that even though beachfront property might be privately owned, when public tax dollars pay for coastal renewal projects, the state may claim ownership of the sand, making the beach open to the public.

Still another beach access dispute ensued in early 1900s Oregon. The then-governor designated the wet sand portion of a beach as public property. Sixty years later developers claimed that the dry portion of the beach belonged to coastal landowners. Hourly tide changes, then, switched public and private ownership back and forth *ad infinitum*. But in 1967, in the most volatile battle in Oregon's legislative history, the "Beach Bill" granted public use up to the vegetation line, which is still a bit obscure.

Determining beach access around the world can be as complicated as the legal jargon surrounding the dispute. No doubt with some ingenuity, non-beachfront property owners who comb the shore for sea glass might be able to blur the often invisible boundaries in their favor. It seems that California's Urban Rangers, with their tape measures and easement maps, are on to something.

Finders Keepers?

For collectors, sea glass might be cherished for the past that it represents. Therein lies another legal situation. Broadly defined and varying from country to country, Antiquities Laws prohibit removing items of interest, such as sea glass, sand, driftwood, and stones from riverbanks and ocean beaches that are part of historic preservation sites. Sea glass is not always free for picking.

To Seed or Not to Seed

The volume of sea glass is diminishing due to environmental laws and the unfortunate invention of plastics. In order to secure the sea glass treasure hunt for future generations, some beachcombers, who shall remain nameless here, seed the ocean with

newly broken glass and shards. Is chucking natural-born elements, such as glass and china, into the ocean considered littering? Probably yes, even though the fragments eventually will make the evolutionary journey back to their original ingredients— sand, soda, and lime. ⌂

Who could resist nature's perfectly created jewelry?
Photo by Maryann Robinson, Marblehead, MA

The Thames riverbanks near London's Tower Bridge offer treasure beyond the wildest imagination.

6
SEA GLASS DESTINATIONS

Mudlarking in the Thames, London, England

"They may be seen of all ages, from mere childhood to positive decrepitude, crawling among the barges at the various wharfs along the river; it cannot be said that they are clad in rags, for they are scarcely half covered by the tattered indescribable things that serve them for clothing; their bodies are grimed with the foul soil of the river, and their torn garments are stiffened up like boards with dirt of every possible description."

This is how journalist Henry Mayhew characterized mudlarks, or riverbank beachcombers, in mid–1800s England. If flourescent orange waders were added to his description, this could be a contemporary scene along the banks of the Thames.

While 18th and 19th century mudlarks scavenged illegally for anything they could sell in order to eek out a meager existence, their modern-day counterparts scan the riverbanks for extraordinary and often museum-worthy artifacts.

Ancient coins, jewelry, metal objects, glass, and crockery have landed in the Thames at least since AD 43 when London was founded. The low oxygen content in the river's thick black mud slows the rate of organic decay and preserves objects that otherwise would have rotted or corroded away. The Port of London Authority owns the Thames riverbed up to the mean high water-mark and allows the public to hunt for treasure only on the shoreline.

But there are real-life dangers to consider while search-ing for history. This tidal river has incoming waves between 16 and 23 feet, and contact with raw sewage and the occa-sional animal carcass are not unheard of. Mudlarking is both grim and fascinating at the same time. It is downright Dickensian.

Steve Brooker, a member of the Thames and Field Mudlarks, says he is "intoxicated by the mud." He has searched the riverbanks for years and found staggering amounts of artifacts. One of his discoveries, a rare 17th century iron ball-and-chain and lock, grabbed worldwide attention.

Brooker, also known as Mud God, works closely with the Museum of London

Mud God Steve Brooker.

and regularly contributes historically significant objects. More interested in puzzling together London's history than finding monetary treasures, Brooker feels a connection to objects with emblems, seals, and signatures. He says, "These pieces identify their former owners, and everybody should have someone to remember them."

Access to the Thames Tube stops: Cannon Street and St. Paul's.

For more information visit: www.thamesandfield2.piczo.com.

Spectacle Island, Boston, MA

After a 15-year cleanup, one of the Boston Harbor Islands has set high standards for turning trash into treasure. Spectacle Island has risen 80 feet above its checkered, environmentally hazardous past and become a model for the future.

The island evolved from a Native American fishing grounds, to a smallpox quarantine station, to housing two hotels that offered, reputedly, gambling and a brothel. It also served as a long-standing dumpsite.

Then the stars aligned. Boston's Central Artery/
Tunnel Project, known as the Big Dig, donated enough
excavated dirt and clay to fill 4,400 barge-loads. This
laid the foundation for the island's transformation.
The addition of two to five feet of topsoil, 28,000 trees
and shrubs, paths, buildings, and a dock "turned the
most environmentally degraded island in the harbor
into the most environmentally friendly," says Bruce
Jacobson, superintendent of Boston Harbor Islands
National Recreation Area.

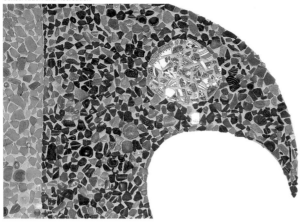

*Mural dedicated to Susan Snow-Cotter, former director of Coastal
Zone Management.*

As a tribute to the island's evolution, artists Carol
Smith-Sloan and Holly Rader of Hingham, MA, created a
wave-patterned mural on one of the island's visitor center's walls. They used approximately 10,000 sea glass and
pottery shards collected on the island.

Sea glass and other artifacts, while plentiful, are
considered cultural resources, and it is illegal to remove
them from the island. Jacobson suggests, "Take only
photos; leave only footprints."

For more information, visit www.nps.gov/boha.

My Favorite Find

It was late May, and one of the first really good minus tides on San Juan Island, Washington. I had just scrambled down the rocks to my favorite little pocket beach, headed right down to the water's edge, and saw this big hunk of glass. My first thought on spotting the insulator was, Oh! Oh! OH! No way! Then I thought, just don't stand there, grab it before a wave comes back in and snatches it! So I threw myself down on the ground, snapped my picture, grabbed my treasure, and did my happy dance. A friend told me that it was probably a neon sign insulator. I am looking forward to going back and hopefully finding more!

—Tami Ewing, Renton, WA

Cape Hatteras Lighthouse, Outer Banks, NC

Nellie Myrtle Pridgen's Beachcomber Museum, Outer Banks, NC

A legendary figure in the Outer Banks, Nellie Myrtle Pridgen fought to protect her once-small fishing village from turning into a multimillion-dollar summer resort. The more she railed against the inevitable property development on the Outer Banks' expansive beaches, the more eccentric she became. She built barriers around her property and cut off contact with her family and friends.

Until her death in 1970, Pridgen continued her solitary walks in search of the ocean's cast-offs that reflect much of the Outer Banks' history. Her house, which once held her parents' grocery store, is now the Nellie Myrtle Pridgen Beachcomber Museum.

Beach treasure in epic proportions crowds shelves, display cases, and floor space. The inventory includes ships' ballast of every conceivable type, Native American peace pipes, whalebones, old fishing tackle, and large amounts of sea glass and shards, including a Bellarmine jug fragment dating to the 16th century. There are also bottles—some containing messages—in this one-of-a-kind museum.

Photo by Shari Hart, Hingham, MA

Pridgen meticulously cataloged each item, and the rooms are much the same as when she left them.

A tribute to her fortitude, the building and museum are listed on the National Register of Historic Places, right up there with the Cape Hatteras Light Station, the Kitty Hawk Life-Saving Station, the USS *Monitor* Shipwreck Site and Remains, and the Wright Brothers National Memorial.

The Nellie Myrtle Pridgen Beachcomber Museum, 4008 South Virginia Dare Trail, Mile Post 13 on the Beach Road, Nags Head.

Virtual Sea Glass Sites:

You'll find lots of sea glass–related topics, including festivals and photo galleries online:

www.seaglassassociation.org
www.seaglasslovers.ning.com
www.odysseyseaglass.com
www.seaglassjournal.com
www.northeastseaglasssociety.ning.com

Naming Names

This list is just a drop in the sand pail. A full accounting of beaches where sea glass can be found, if it were possible, which it isn't, would probably fill several books.

Many collectors will be amused that I have overlooked or omitted their favorite beaches. Others might feel betrayed because I named theirs. There are two schools of thought about revealing sea glass beaches, and the rules of etiquette are roundly discussed on sea glass websites. I have chosen the karma approach.

The following list aside, keep in mind that today's sea glass–laden beach might be barren tomorrow. I have not visited many of these regions, but friends have contributed additional information. Still I cannot verify the accuracy.

I know that I go against the current when I say: rest assured, there will be plenty of sea glass for future generations. Consider the strength of storms ripping back sand and pushing it forward, combined with shifting tides and the moon's gravitational effects. There are centuries' worth of sea glass and shards hiding, resting, traveling. It's got to turn up somewhere.

These intaglios, which are carved in sunken-relief, were once part of a ring, circa 1800s. They were found on the Thames foreshore.

United States

Alabama

Dauphin Island

Gulfport

Alaska

Aleutian Islands

Jewel Beach, Kodiak

California

Davenport

Main Boardwalk

Beach, Santa Cruz

Monterey

San Francisco Bay

Sand City, Monterey

Bay

Santa Barbara

Seaside State Beach,

Monterey

Connecticut

Hammonasset Beach

State Park,

Madison

New London

Delaware

Bethany Beach

Cape Henlopen State
Park, Lewes

Rehoboth Beach

Florida

Delray Beach

Siesta Key

Vero Beach

Hawaii

Ala Moana Beach,
Oahu

Glass Beach, Kauai

Hanapepe Town
Harbor, Kauai

Illinois

Glencoe Beach,
Glencoe

Kenilworth Beach,
Kenilworth

Maple Park Beach,

Winnetka

Northwestern
University Beach

Maryland

Cape Charles

Chesapeake Bay

Deal Island

Kent Island

Potomac River

Susquehanna River

Massachusetts

George's Island

Marblehead

Nantasket Beach, Hull

Provincetown

Scituate

Spectacle Island

Ten Pound Island

Maine

Bar Island, Bar Harbor

Cranberry Islands

Deer Isle

Eastport

Monhegan Island

Mount Desert Island

York

Michigan

Conger-Lighthouse
    Beach, Port Huron

Magoon Creek,
    Manistee

Van Buren Beach,
    South Haven

Mississippi

Horn Island

Ship Island

New Jersey

Sunset Beach, Cape
    May

New York

Crescent Beach,
    Glen Cove

Fire Island

Hudson River,
    Grand View

North Shore,
    Long Island

Southern side of Lake
    Ontario, Rochester

North Carolina

Outer Banks

Ohio

Conneaut

Huntington Beach,
    Cleveland

Walnut Beach,
    Ashtabula

Oregon

Astoria

Newport

Siletz Bay, Lincoln
    City

Pennsylvania

Presque Isle, Erie

Rhode Island

Easton's Beach, Newport

Sandy Point Beach,
Portsmouth

South Carolina

Cherry Grove Beach

Murrells Inlet

Texas

West Beach, Galveston

Virginia

Ocean View Beach,
Norfolk

Cape Charles

Washington

Alki Beach, Seattle

Glass Beach, Port
Townsend

Rosario Beach, Fidalgo
Island

West Beach, Whidbey
Island

Australia

Brighton Beach,
Melbourne

Boomer Beach,
Adelaide

Kurnell Beach, Botany
Bay

Main Beach, Wollongong

Belize

Coco Plum Island

Bermuda

Achilles Bay Beach

Glass Beach,
Buildings Bay,
St. George

Alexander Battery Park
Beach

Canada

Beau Bois Beach, New
Labrador, Nova Scotia
Myrick's Shore, Prince
Edward Island
Beresford Beach, New
Brunswick
Scarborough Bluffs,
Ontario

Caribbean

Aguadilla, Puerto Rico
Bastiamento Beach,
Vieques, Puerto
Rico
Chileno Bay, Cabo San
Lucas, Mexico
Domes Beach, Rincon,

Puerto Rico
Guana Island,
British Virgin
Islands
Hawksbill Rock,
Antigua
Mazatlan, Mexico
Montego Bay, Jamaica
Nassau, New
Providence Island,
Bahamas
Natural Pool, Aruba
North Pointe, Cayman
Islands
Palm/Eagle Beach,
Aruba
Pals Beach, Girona,
Mexico
Playa la Media Luna,
Isla

Mujeres, Mexico

Seven Mile Beach,
Cayman Islands

Southern Abaco
Island, Bahamas

Tahiti Beach, Abaco
Island, Bahamas

Virgin Gorda, British
Virgin Islands

England

Isle of Wight

Isles of Scilly

Lyme Regis

Morecambe Bay,
Lancashire

Pentewan Beach,
Cornwall

France

Antibes

La Rochelle

Mont St. Michele

St. Malo

Greece

Aegina

Andros

Santorini

Holland

Island of Texel

The Hague, south side
of the harbor

Ireland

Derrymore Strand

Kearney Beach,
    Kearney

Rathlin Island

Israel

Akko, Mediterranean
    shore

Red Sea

Italy

Amalfi Coast

Ponza Island

Positano

Japan

Mutsu Bay, Honshu
    Island

White Beach, Okinawa

Scotland

Fife

Inverness

Isle of Iona, Argyll

North Berwick

Tralee Bay

Wales

Colwyn Bay

Porth Swtan

Thanks to the following experts and friends for their generous contributions: Gay Bogard, Debby Boone, Marilyn Boyles, Terry Bregy, Steve Brooker of Thames and Field Mudlarks, Pembroke S. Bryant, Muriel Burnheimer, Linda Callahan, Camden Public Library, Pauline Carver, Lynda Chilton, Dodie Clarke, Londi Colton, Ian Cox, Christie Cummins, Ginger Dolham, Denise Donnelly, Steve Dumas, Anne Dunbar, Curt Ebbesmeyer, Tami Ewing, Sherry Fields, JoAnna Forrester, Val Guarin, Gary Harriman, Shari Hart, Linda Jereb, Dawna Hilton, Kirsti and Jonathan Hoover, Anthony Hutcheson at Right Click Computers, Bruce Jacobson of the National Park Service, Cyndee Hilliard, Tina Lam, Richard LaMotte, Linda Leonard, Sean McMinn, Laura Meade, Ari Meil, Michael Morrissey, Vivian Morosi, James L. Nelson, Jessica Renehan of the Massachusetts Department of Conservation and Recreation, Vicki Roberts, Maryann C. Robinson, Joan & Tom Sabatino, Sharon Sand, Ariadne Skyrianidou, Sue Smith, Michael Steere, Melinda Vahradian, Kaja Veilleux, John Viehman, Wyatt Shorey, Dawn White, Sandy Whitney, Chaz Winkler, Karin Womer, and Lynne Wood.